The FBI

CORNERSTONES OF FREEDOM
SECOND SERIES

Sarah De Capua

Children's Press®
A Division of Scholastic Inc.
New York • Toronto • London • Auckland • Sydney
Mexico City • New Delhi • Hong Kong
Danbury, Connecticut

Photographs © 2002: AP/Wide World Photos/Linda Spillers: 25; Brown Brothers: 5, 7 left, 11, 18; Corbis Images: 15 bottom, 19, 44 center right (Bettmann), 39 (Henry Diltz), 4 (Larry Downing/Reuters), 3 (Doug Kanter/AFP), 36 (Larry Lee Photography), cover bottom (Robert Maass), 33 bottom; Corbis Sygma/Seanna O'Sullivan: 45 top right; Folio, Inc.: 8, 20, 24, 29 (Rob Crandall), 16 (Elias Goldensky), 21, 45 top left (Jim Pickerell), 13; Hulton Archive/Getty Images: 33 top (Jim Bourg/Reuters), 35 (Hamid Mir/Editor/Reuters/Ausaf Newspaper for Daily Dawn), 6, 7 right, 10, 15 top, 44 top left, 44 top right; Photri Inc.: 22 (Mark E. Gibson), 14, 17, 27, 38, 44 bottom left; The Image Works: 23, 37, 44 bottom right (Rob Crandall), 30 (Johnny Crawford), 32 (Bob Daemmrich); Woodfin Camp & Associates: 12 (Yousuf Karsh), cover top (J. Marmaras), 26, 28, 45 bottom (Frank Muller-May).

Library of Congress Cataloging-in-Publication Data

De Capua, Sarah.
  The FBI / Sarah De Capua.
      p. cm.—(Cornerstones of freedom. Second series)
Published simultaneously in Canada.
Summary: Introduces the history and function of the Federal Bureau of Investigation, and presents facts about such topics as women and minorities in the Bureau, the FBI Academy, and how to become an agent.
Includes bibliographical references and index.
   ISBN 0-516-22691-6
   1. United States. Federal Bureau of Investigation—Juvenile literature. [1. United States. Federal Bureau of Investigation.]
I.Title. II. Series.
HV8144.F43 D4 2002
363.25'0973—dc21

                              2002001535

1 2 3 4 5 6 7 8 9 10 R 11 10 09 08 07 06 05 04 03 02

EVERY DAY FOR MORE than six months, dump trucks brought eight thousand tons of rubble from the World Trade Center's twin towers to a dump on Staten Island, across the Hudson River from Manhattan. The twin towers were destroyed on September 11, 2001, when terrorists **hijacked** two airplanes and flew them into the buildings.

Agents from the Federal Bureau of Investigation (FBI) carefully sifted through the mountains of rubble looking for evidence. They already knew how the buildings had collapsed. They looked for evidence that would tell them why. Did the metal support beams of the buildings melt from the heat of the raging fires, causing them to collapse? They looked for parts of the planes that crashed into the buildings and for clues about the terrorists.

COCKPIT VOICE RECORDERS

FBI agents in Washington, D.C., studied the cockpit voice recorders from two of the four planes hijacked on September 11, 2001. These devices record everything that the pilots in the cockpit say. Cockpit voice recorders provide valuable information after a crash.

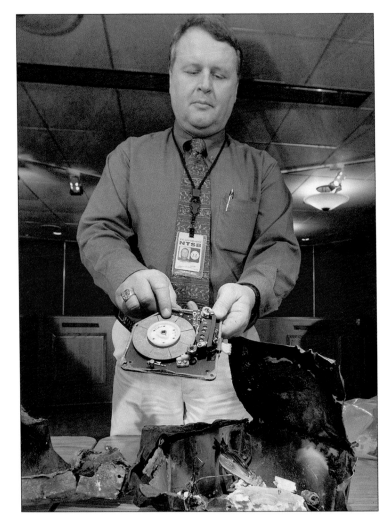

Cockpit voice recorders like this one help FBI investigators figure out what happens when a plane crashes.

Founded in 1908, the FBI is the investigative arm of the United States Department of Justice, the chief law-enforcement branch of the United States government. The FBI is a powerful agency with almost unlimited resources to enforce **federal** laws—laws set up by the national government—and to protect the nation's security.

Allan Pinkerton, founder of the Pinkerton National Detective Agency

THE PINKERTONS

Before there were FBI agents, there were Pinkertons. Private detective agencies were responsible for national law enforcement prior to the establishment of the FBI. The Pinkerton National Detective Agency, founded in 1850 by Allan Pinkerton, was the first, largest, and most successful of these agencies. By 1866, the agency had offices in New York City and Philadelphia, Pennsylvania, and employed about eighty agents. At first, the railroads were the agency's main clients. In addition to policing trains, the Pinkertons, as the agency's men became known, were assigned to catch and arrest train robbers. During the 1870s, the detectives hunted down bank robbers and guarded companies' property during strikes. A strike is when unhappy workers stop working and demand better conditions from their employers.

By 1884, the Pinkerton National Detective Agency had offices throughout the United States. It offered security, investigative, and law-enforcement services to private businesses, such as factories and stores. It also offered intelligence services, or ways to obtain information about an enemy, and counterintelligence. Counterintelligence involves activity that is designed to block an enemy from obtaining information, as well as gathering political and military information about an enemy. The

ALLAN PINKERTON

Allan Pinkerton was born in 1819 in Glasgow, Scotland. He immigrated to the United States in 1845, and settled near Chicago, Illinois. In 1848, Pinkerton became sheriff of Kane County, Illinois. Soon after, he moved to Chicago to become a private detective. Two years later he established the Pinkerton National Detective Agency. Pinkerton died in Chicago on July 1, 1884.

5

Pinkertons provided these services to government agencies. The U.S. Treasury Department hired Pinkertons to find gangs of counterfeiters—people who make fake money. The U.S. Post Office used Pinkertons to solve cases of mail theft. The Pinkerton National Detective Agency was the only national detective agency until 1908, when the Bureau of Investigation was founded.

THE MODERN DAY FBI IS FOUNDED

In 1908, President Theodore Roosevelt was troubled by the illegal sale of land in the American West. He wanted to arrest and punish the people responsible. The Department of Justice had the power to stop the illegal land sales, but it did not employ enough people to investigate the crimes and to arrest suspects, or people thought to have committed a crime. President Roosevelt ordered **Attorney General** Charles J. Bonaparte to create an investigative service within the Justice Department. On July 26, 1908, Bonaparte issued an order that allowed the Justice Department to hire a small group of detectives.

President Theodore Roosevelt

Attorney General Charles J. Bonaparte, who gave the Justice Department the ability to do detective work

President William Howard Taft

By 1909, while William Howard Taft was president, the group was officially named the Bureau of Investigation. In 1935, Congress, the lawmaking body of the United States, changed the bureau's name to the Federal Bureau of Investigation.

THE FBI'S ROLE

Today's FBI is responsible for investigating crimes related to more than three hundred federal laws. These laws deal with several violent crimes, such as kidnapping and terrorism, as well as **espionage,** or spying that takes place within the United States. The FBI also gathers evidence in crimes called **felonies**, such as when a suspect crosses state lines. Other examples of felonies are hate crimes, and certain kinds of racial **discrimination.**

The FBI also investigates organized crime. People who engage in organized crime belong to formal groups that are well coordinated to carry out their activities. Well-known organized crime groups are the Italian Mafia, the Japanese Yakuza, and the Taiwanese United Bamboo.

The official seal of the Federal Bureau of Investigation

EARLY RESPONSIBILITIES AND CHALLENGES

During its first years, the bureau's responsibilities grew quickly. It was responsible for enforcing federal laws and catching suspects who moved across state lines to avoid being **prosecuted,** or having legal action carried out against them. For a while in the United States, something that was a crime in one state might not have been a crime in another state. Sometimes, a person who committed a crime fled to a state where that action was not illegal. If the suspect succeeded in reaching another state, it usually took a long time for law-enforcement officials in the states to work out the details of returning the suspect to the state where he or she would be charged with the crime. Laws in the United States have changed over the years, making it easier to capture suspects, even if they flee across state lines.

However, the bureau had many problems. It was not well organized and had no central leadership. Agents were not required to follow specific rules of behavior. The Department of Justice could not control its agents because they were scattered across the country, far from the department's headquarters in Washington, D.C. As a result, many agents were influenced by local politicians. Sometimes the politicians paid the agents to ignore them when they broke the law.

THE DEPARTMENT OF JUSTICE

Founded in 1870, the Department of Justice is located in Washington, D.C. It is responsible for enforcing and prosecuting the laws of the United States. Agents in the FBI, which is a part of the Department of Justice, track and catch people who break the laws. Then lawyers who work for the Department of Justice prosecute those people in the nation's courts.

Thousands gather in Red Square to listen to speeches during the Russian Revolution of 1917.

In 1917, the United States entered World War I (1914–18), and at this time the Bureau of Investigation employed four hundred men. After the Russian Revolution of 1917, when **communists** took control of Russia, the bureau began investigating suspected American communists because they were considered enemies of the United States. During the years after World War I, the bureau worked successfully to break the power of the white supremacist organization called the Ku Klux Klan (KKK). (White supremacists believe that the white race is mentally, physically, and emotionally superior to other races.)

* * * *

THE J. EDGAR HOOVER YEARS

In 1924, J. Edgar Hoover became the director of the Bureau of Investigation. The twenty-nine-year-old Hoover had been appointed assistant director of the bureau in 1921, after working as an assistant to the U.S. attorney general. At the time Hoover became director, many Americans thought the bureau should be disbanded, or broken up. Some of the bureau's agents had been involved in government **scandals** and illegal activities. Hoover believed the public's opinion of the bureau would improve if he made changes. Hoover

The Ku Klux Klan was one of the organizations targeted by the FBI.

J. Edgar Hoover, director of the FBI from 1924 to 1972

sent agents throughout the country a long list of rules and guidelines. The agents were required to behave responsibly and professionally. They were reminded that their only duty was to investigate violations of federal laws.

The FBI Identification Division has 250 million fingerprints on file.

FINGERPRINTS ON FILE

In 1924, Congress created the bureau's Identification Division. At the time, more than eight hundred thousand fingerprints were sent to the bureau's Washington, D.C., headquarters from the Bureau of Criminal Identification in Chicago, Illinois, and the U.S. **Penitentiary** in Leavenworth, Kansas. The Identification Division enables local police throughout the country to identify criminals who have committed crimes in other places. This is important because if a person has committed the same crime in more than one place, he or she may be charged with a more serious crime. As a result, the person may receive a tougher punishment if convicted.

Agents were fired if they used brutality, or cruel and excessive force, during an investigation; drank alcohol while working; or used a government-issued car for anything other than official business. Hoover reviewed the file

This man is examining a gun under a microscope at the FBI lab.

of every agent in the bureau and fired anyone who was unfair or did not perform his job well.

Hoover hired agents with college degrees, usually in law or accounting. He established uniform rules so that every agent in the country would conduct investigations the same way. Hoover also created the FBI National Academy, a school to train new **recruits** and local police officers from throughout the country in bureau methods. He established the huge FBI laboratory, which continues to bring the latest advances in scientific research to crime fighting.

As the years passed, bureau agents were given more responsibilities. Congress gave agents the power to carry guns. Agents' work in the 1930s helped to end the careers of well-known **gangsters** such as John Dillinger and Charles "Pretty Boy" Floyd. Agents began investigating bank robberies, kidnappings, **blackmail,** and other criminal activities.

In 1950, Hoover created the FBI's Ten Most Wanted list, which helps to publicize especially dangerous suspects. The list includes the names and photographs of the ten criminals the FBI would most like to capture. By making the list available at places such as post offices, the FBI enlists the public's help in locating the suspects. If a person spots someone from the list, he or she should call the police. The list is also available online at fbi.gov/mostwant/topten/tenlist.htm.

The FBI brought gangsters such as John Dillinger (above) and Charles "Pretty Boy" Floyd (below) to justice.

15

G-MEN

Under J. Edgar Hoover the FBI became one of the most popular government agencies during the 1940s. FBI agents were called G-men (the G stood for government), and they were considered to be heroes. Children played games in which they pretended to be FBI agents who chased and captured "bad guys." Many boys wore "junior G-man" pajamas to bed at night.

President Franklin D. Roosevelt

Hoover was the bureau's director for forty-eight years, until his death in 1972. During that time the agency became one of the world's largest and most respected investigative bureaus.

THE FBI AFTER WORLD WAR II

In 1936, prior to World War II, President Franklin Roosevelt gave secret orders to the bureau to investigate communist activity in the United States. The end of World War II (1939–45) brought more changes to the FBI. Agents more vigorously investigated people in the United States who were believed to be communists. J. Edgar Hoover was strongly anticommunist and used the bureau's resources to expose as many communists as possible.

In the late 1940s and 1950s many communist spies were caught. Some of these spies were involved in stealing secret information about how to build atomic bombs. The United States dropped an atomic bomb on the Japanese cities of Hiroshima and Nagasaki in August 1945 to end World War II. It was important to the United States that information on how to build an atomic bomb remain secret, and not fall into the hands of countries that would use atomic bombs against this country.

The atomic bomb explosion in Hiroshima, Japan, on August 6, 1945

Some people, though, believed that the bureau violated the civil rights of many of the people it investigated. They thought the FBI looked into the background of citizens who had not committed any crimes. They disagreed with Director Hoover's anticommunist views. Others did not trust the

FBI. They claimed that agents were listening in on people's telephone conversations, opening people's mail, and even breaking into and searching people's homes. Some of these accusations were true.

Others, however, believed the FBI did a great service for the United States by ending the careers of many genuine communist spies. They were also grateful to the FBI for exposing communist organizations that may have sought to damage the U.S. government and its citizens.

THE CIVIL RIGHTS MOVEMENT AND THE FBI

In 1957, while Dwight D. Eisenhower was president, Congress passed the first of many laws to protect Americans' civil rights, especially those of minorities. The FBI became responsible for enforcing the federal civil rights laws. Hoover said the laws were important "to ensure that no citizen is deprived of the free exercise or enjoyment of any right or privilege secured to him by the Constitution."

The FBI has been the focus of **debate** over how successfully it has met its goals to protect civil rights. The bureau's agents have sometimes abused their power by setting illegal **wiretaps** and engaging in

President Dwight D. Eisenhower

18

* * * *

unlawful burglaries and even kidnappings. New rules were established in 1975 to prevent such activities from occurring in the future. The bureau accepted the rules willingly. It stopped illegal practices of investigation and has worked hard to restore its reputation as a protector of civil rights.

L. Patrick Gray, who took over as director of the FBI after Hoover's death

WOMEN AND MINORITIES IN THE FBI

When J. Edgar Hoover died in 1972, there were only 145 minority agents and no women in a total force of 8,659 agents employed by the FBI. After Hoover's death, L. Patrick Gray was appointed director. Gray allowed women to become FBI agents for the first time. However, there still were few women and people of color working in the FBI.

THE NATIONAL CRIME INFORMATION CENTER

In 1967, the National Crime Information Center (NCIC) was established at FBI headquarters in Washington, D.C. Today the system is called NCIC 2000, and it is the world's largest computerized information center. The NCIC maintains millions of files on criminals and criminal activities. Electronically stored data can be recovered quickly. As a result, FBI records can be used to assist local police throughout the country within minutes of a request for information. NCIC 2000 can download information directly to patrol cars and mobile police officers. This enables law enforcers to identify and capture suspects more quickly.

★ ★ ★ ★

In 1980, the bureau made the inclusion of women and minorities one of its top goals. The bureau wanted to have a force made up of agents that more closely represented the American population. The bureau also began to appreciate the unique contributions that women and minorities would make to law enforcement.

Today there are about 11,500 agents in the FBI. About 1,700 of them are women. Approximately 1,500 agents are black, Hispanic, Asian, or American Indian.

These women are doing a 2-mile (3.2-kilometer) run as part of their FBI physical training.

The J. Edgar Hoover FBI Building in Washington, D.C.

THE J. EDGAR HOOVER BUILDING

Completed in 1975, the J. Edgar Hoover Building houses the national headquarters of the FBI. The building is located on Pennsylvania Avenue and E Street in Washington, D.C., and covers one city block. It is seven stories high on Pennsylvania Avenue and eleven stories high on E Street, providing offices and work space for more than nine hundred FBI agents and six thousand other employees.

The large flowerpots in front of the FBI Building protect it from car bombs.

Some of the world's most high-tech laboratories are also found here. In these laboratories about five hundred scientists, technicians, and other experts analyze evidence to help solve crimes. Here they study blood, hair, fibers, teeth, skin, and body fluids. They also analyze bullets, knives, firearms, metals and rocks, handwriting, papers, inks, and anything else that could be part of a crime investigation.

The FBI laboratories do not work only on FBI investigations. The scientists also analyze evidence for local and state police departments throughout the country. Their test results are used in local cases when criminals are brought to trial. Sometimes FBI experts testify at these trials.

Employees and official visitors to the J. Edgar Hoover Building use computer-controlled identification badges to enter. Non-FBI employees must enter and exit the building through a separate door. They must walk through a metal detector and have their belongings x-rayed. To protect the building from car bombs, large concrete objects designed as huge flowerpots surround the entire building. If a bomb exploded, the concrete would absorb the explosion and lessen damage to the building and the people who work inside. Heavy gates protect the driveways leading to the building.

THE FBI NATIONAL ACADEMY

Even larger than the J. Edgar Hoover Building is the FBI National Academy in Quantico, Virginia, about 40 miles (64 km) south of Washington, D.C. The academy includes twenty-one buildings, which cover 385 acres (156 hectares).

Men and women who want to become FBI agents are trained here after they pass a written test and an interview with a group of agents. Experienced agents and thousands of law-enforcement officers from throughout the United States go to the academy to receive special training in new crime-fighting techniques.

The academy's buildings include **dormitories,** class-rooms, and research areas, as well as an auditorium, library, gymnasium, weight room, and indoor swimming pool. The site

The FBI National Academy in Quantico, Virginia

THE HALL OF HONOR

The Hall of Honor is located in the administration building of the FBI National Academy. It honors past directors of the FBI. One wall contains a plaque that pays tribute to all the men and women of the FBI. Another plaque honors FBI agents who gave their lives in the line of duty. A section of the Hall of Honor is dedicated to police officers from all over the country who graduated from the academy and later lost their lives in the line of duty.

features indoor and outdoor shooting ranges for target practice, a track, and tennis courts. A make-believe town called Hogan's Alley is used for training purposes. There agents learn techniques for arrests, searches, rescues, and captures.

Training for FBI agents at the National Academy takes sixteen weeks. However, top law-enforcement officers from all over the world may be invited to attend a special twelve-week program just for them.

The latest crime-fighting techniques are taught at the FBI National Academy.

The sign for Hogan's Alley on the grounds of the FBI National Academy

PROFILERS

The study of evidence does not take place only in the FBI's laboratories. A special kind of study of evidence is done at the FBI National Academy by people called profilers.

These experts gather all of the available information about a particular crime. They study the information and compare it to similar crimes that have been solved and the people who committed them. The profilers put all of the information together to figure out what the person who committed the crime is probably like. This is called a profile. The profile may contain the criminal's gender,

Fingerprints are just one of the types of information that the FBI stores to help law-enforcement officers around the country catch criminals.

age, job, hobbies, degree of education, where he or she lives, and more. The profiles these experts develop can help police search for suspects.

THE FBI'S CLEARINGHOUSE

The Criminal Justice Information Service is the branch of the FBI that acts as a clearinghouse, or center, for information about crimes, suspects, victims, and evidence. It provides that information to FBI field offices, as well as to local and state police, throughout the country.

The FBI gathers and stores an enormous amount of information. The FBI's file index has about eighty million names. It adds one million more every fourteen months.

The 250 million sets of fingerprints the bureau keeps come mostly from criminals, or suspected criminals, who have been arrested and fingerprinted by law-enforcement agencies throughout the country. The rest come from people applying for military, teaching, or other jobs that require fingerprinting as part of the application process.

The agency also stores millions of identification numbers from cars, guns, and other objects that might be stolen, as well as millions of more pieces of information about missing persons, unidentified victims, and suspects.

Even a serial number ground off of a weapon can be restored by the FBI.

27

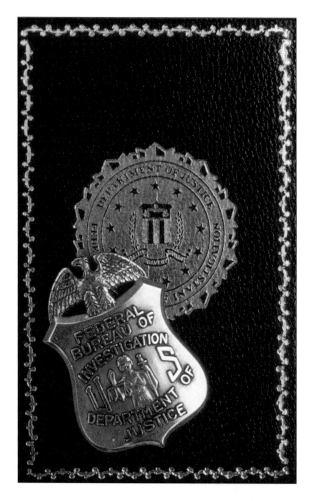

SECURITY CHECK

The security check looks into an applicant's background

to ensure that he or she has never been convicted

of a serious crime, such as burglary or murder, and has

a good character. Part of the security check includes

the applicant's being fingerprinted and passing a

lie-detector test.

DO YOU WANT TO BE AN FBI AGENT?

About one of every eleven FBI agents works at FBI headquarters in Washington, D.C. The rest work at FBI field offices throughout the country.

Becoming an agent is not easy. Each year, the FBI receives between five thousand and eleven thousand applications. Of those, the bureau accepts only three hundred to five hundred agents. **Applicants** must be U.S. citizens who are highly intelligent and in good physical condition. They must be drug free, be able to pass a security check, and hold a four-year college degree.

A person who wants to become an FBI agent can apply when he or she is as young as twenty-three or as old as thirty-seven. Most of those who are accepted, however, are between thirty and thirty-five because the FBI wants men and women who have already gained years of experience working in a related field. That experience does not have to be in law enforcement. It may be in business, engineering, the military, the law, the computer industry, or one of many other areas of expertise the FBI needs to help it fight crime.

Good physical condition is a requirement for FBI agents.

COMPUTER CRIME

The 1990s brought the Internet into homes, schools, and public libraries. The Internet brought a new challenge to the FBI—online computer crime. This includes crimes against children. Federal laws prohibit, or forbid, using computers to lure children into immoral and dangerous activities.

In 1995, the FBI conducted a legal search of the homes of 120 people in Miami, Florida; Dallas, Texas; and New York City. The people were suspected of being involved in attracting children to engage in illegal acts. The investigation that

The FBI protects children from online computer crime so that they can feel safe going to the Internet to do homework.

led to the searches took two years to complete. It involved undercover agents who posed as minors, or people who are under the age of eighteen. Other agents used the same computer services as the suspects in order to gather evidence against them. Today, the FBI continues to investigate serious crimes, including **hacking**, that involve computers.

DOMESTIC TERRORISM

Terrorism that occurs in the United States is called domestic terrorism. The FBI is the leading law-enforcement agency that studies acts of domestic terrorism and identifies the people responsible for committing them.

On February 26, 1993, a car bomb in an underground garage at New York City's World Trade Center exploded, leaving a crater five stories deep. The explosion killed six people, injured more than one thousand, and trapped thousands of office workers inside the twin towers.

The following day, three hundred FBI agents and an FBI bomb squad arrived in New York City from Washington, D.C. Their work led to the arrest, trial, and conviction of several Muslim extremists, or Muslims who are dedicated to the destruction of those who do not share their beliefs.

In Oklahoma City, Oklahoma, a truck containing a bomb was parked in front of the Alfred P. Murrah Federal Building on April 19, 1995. The truck exploded and the blast destroyed an entire side of the Murrah building, collapsing the floors within. Several buildings nearby were damaged, and the blast was felt 30 miles (48 km) away. The explosion killed 168 people and injured 850 others.

The Alfred P. Murrah Federal Building in Oklahoma City, after it was destroyed by a truck bomb

More than five hundred FBI agents investigated the case. Within days the FBI identified an American, Timothy McVeigh, as the prime suspect. McVeigh was antigovernment, which was why he targeted the federal building, a place where hundreds of government employees worked. Shortly after, another American, Terry Nichols, was also identified as a suspect. Both McVeigh and Nichols were arrested, tried separately, and convicted of the terrorist bombing. McVeigh was sentenced to death. The sentence was carried out on June 11, 2001. Nichols received a sentence of life in prison without **parole**, or early release.

Between 1978 and 1996 a total of sixteen bombings were committed by one person. Some of the bombs were sent by mail. One bomb went off on an airplane. Other bombs were left in public places, often at universities. All together, the bombings killed three people and injured twenty-three in eight states.

For eighteen years, the FBI investigated the case. Finally, in 1996, American Theodore Kaczynski, the so-called Unabomber, was arrested. Kaczynski was found living in a remote cabin in Montana. Before Kaczynski could go to trial, he pleaded guilty. Kaczynski did not believe that technology, or scientific advances to improve life, was good. He targeted universities and airlines because of their regular use of and encouragement of the use of technology. He received a sentence of life in prison without parole.

Timothy McVeigh, who was convicted of the Oklahoma City terrorist bombing and put to death for the crime

Theodore Kaczynski, escorted by two FBI agents, was convicted of being the Unabomber in 1996.

THE UNABOMBER

The bomber's first targets were universities and airlines. As a result, the FBI used the first letters of those words to name its investigation UNABOM. They referred to the person committing the bombing crimes as the Unabomber.

★ ★ ★ ★

At 8:46 A.M. on September 11, 2001, an American Airlines jet flew into the north tower of New York City's World Trade Center. At 9:03 A.M., a United Airlines jet flew into the World Trade Center's south tower. At 9:38 A.M., an American Airlines jet crashed into the Pentagon, the headquarters of the U.S. military near Washington, D.C. A second United Airlines jet crashed in a field near Shanksville, Pennsylvania, at 10:06 A.M. That plane may have been headed toward the White House or the Capitol building in Washington, D.C. All four of the jet planes were hijacked by Muslim extremists. The attacks, the worst in U.S. history, killed approximately three thousand people.

Within hours of the attacks, the FBI released the names of nineteen suspects who likely carried out the hijackings. Their leader, Osama bin Laden, a Saudi Arabian living in Afghanistan, is responsible for numerous terrorist attacks throughout the world.

THE FBI AFTER SEPTEMBER 11, 2001

Immediately following the September 11 attacks, the FBI had a new crime to focus on. In September and October 2001, four dangerous letters were mailed to government offices, postal facilities, and news organizations. The letters were dangerous because they contained **bacteria** that cause a disease called anthrax. People who contract anthrax can die if they are not treated quickly with medicine. A total of seventeen people got sick with anthrax. Five people died.

Terrorist Osama bin Laden, whose al Qaeda network was responsible for the attacks on the United States that occurred on September 11, 2001

FBI scientists were able to take samples of the bacteria and study them. They also studied the letters for clues to the identity of the person who sent them. Two of the letters were sent to lawmakers in Washington, D.C., who work in the Capitol, where the nation's laws are made. FBI agents examined more than six hundred bags that contained mail addressed to other people in the Capitol. The agents were looking for more letters that might have contained anthrax bacteria.

The FBI believes the anthrax letters were acts of domestic terrorism. The FBI and the United States Postal Service offered a reward of more than $2 million to anyone who could provide information that would lead to the arrest and conviction of the person responsible for sending the letters.

Another important goal since September 11, 2001, is hiring more people who speak foreign languages to work for the bureau. Since terrorists can be found all over the world, it is important for FBI agents to be able to communicate with people in other countries to get information about terrorists and their activities. The FBI is seeking people who speak Chinese, Hebrew, Russian, Farsi, and other languages. The people, called linguists, may work as special agents, assisting the FBI with translation and interviews. Anyone hired as an FBI linguist must meet all the other requirements for employment by the FBI.

The FBI does not just contribute investigative skills to crimes and terrorism. Perhaps one of the FBI's most important contributions is its Community Outreach Program (COP). For years, the FBI has maintained COP as a way to keep the public informed about crime prevention and personal safety.

The Pentagon in Arlington, Virginia, after the attack on September 11, 2001

★　　★　　★　　★

The Community Outreach Program is made up of FBI employees who work with national and local community organizations and law-enforcement agencies. They volunteer their time to set up awareness and prevention programs for students and communities. These programs usually relate to crime, drugs, and violence. Since the September 11 attacks on the United States, COP has focused more on terrorism and on being prepared for emergencies.

Barbara Wallace is the unit chief of the Community Outreach Program at FBI headquarters in Washington, D.C. She says, "The FBI's COP program is working with communities, schools, businesses, and religious organizations to increase awareness." Since the attacks, COP presentations have explained what terrorism is, its history, and how

Contaminated mail has been a major issue since the September 11, 2001 attacks.

it relates to current events. Presenters have included tips on how to handle suspicious mail, how to respond to emergencies, and how to increase personal safety. For example, COP presenters stress that everyone should know or carry with them emergency telephone numbers. Emergency numbers include those for the local hospital, police station, or fire station.

COP has reached out specifically to young people. The FBI recognized that everyone, including students, wanted to help out after the September 11 terrorist attacks. COP presenters show students that they can do something every day to make a difference. For example, they can help other students who lost a parent or relative in the attacks. Members of community organizations who volunteer for the outreach program also talk about the attacks, listen to students' concerns, and provide ways for them to discuss their fears.

FBI field offices throughout the country are working with local organizations to find the best ways to reach people in specific communities. Meanwhile, thousands of students participate in the free program every year.

THE IMPORTANCE OF THE FBI

During the FBI's existence, its most notable cases have involved important events in U.S. history. Such cases illustrate the FBI's important place in American society. In the future the FBI will continue to play a leading role in U.S. law enforcement.

FBI Directors

Stanley W. Finch	1908–1912
Alexander Bruce Bielaski	1912–1919
William E. Allen	1919
William J. Flynn	1919–1921
William J. Burns	1921–1924
J. Edgar Hoover	1924–1972
L. Patrick Gray	1972–1973
William D. Ruckelshaus	1973
Clarence M. Kelley	1973–1978
William H. Webster	1978–1987
John Otto	1987
William S. Sessions	1987–1993
Floyd I. Clarke	1993
Louis J. Freeh	1993–2001
Thomas J. Pickard	2001
Robert S. Mueller, III	2001–

Glossary

attorney general—the top law-enforcement officer in the United States

bacteria—microscopic living things that exist all around you. Many bacteria are useful, but some cause disease.

blackmail—the crime of threatening to reveal a secret about someone unless the person pays a sum of money or grants a favor

communists—people who support communism, a way of organizing a country so that all land, houses, and resources belong to the government and the profits are shared by all the people of that country

debate—a discussion between two sides with different views

discrimination—prejudice or unjust behavior toward others based on differences in age, race, gender, ethnicity, or other factors

dormitories—buildings with many separate sleeping rooms

espionage—spying that takes place within the United States to gain political secrets

federal—having to do with the national government

felonies—serious crimes because of the punishment involved if found guilty. The punishment may be more than one year of imprisonment or death.

gangsters—members of a criminal gang

hacking—breaking into a computer system illegally

hijacked—taken over by force

penitentiary—a state or federal prison for people found guilty of serious crimes

prosecuted—carried out a legal action in a court of law against a person accused of a crime

recruits—people who have recently joined a group or organization

scandals—dishonest or immoral acts that shock people and disgrace those involved

wiretap—a listening device on a telephone that allows others to overhear conversations

Timeline: The FBI

1850	1908	1921	1924	1930s	1935	1936
The Pinkerton National Detective Agency is founded.	The Bureau of Investigation is founded.	J. Edgar Hoover becomes assistant director of the Bureau of Investigation. Congress creates the bureau's Identification Division.	Hoover becomes director of the Bureau of Investigation.	  Bureau agents end the careers of well-known gangsters, including John Dillinger and Charles "Pretty Boy" Floyd.	Congress changes bureau's name to the Federal Bureau of Investigation. The FBI National Academy is established in Quantico, Virginia.	President Franklin D. Roosevelt gives secret order to bureau to investigate communists in the United States.

44

A series of bombings later known to be committed by Theodore Kaczynski begins.

A truck bomb explodes at the Murrah Federal Building in Oklahoma City, Oklahoma.

Theodore Kaczynski captured as the Unabomber.

Timothy McVeigh is put to death for his role in the Oklahoma City bombing.

The National Crime Information Center is established.

J. Edgar Hoover dies.

The FBI National Academy moves to a larger area of Quantico, Virginia.

The J. Edgar Hoover Building becomes the new headquarters of the FBI.

Terrorist attacks kill approximately 3,000 people in New York City, Arlington, Virginia, and Pennsylvania.

To Find Out More

BOOKS

D'Angelo, Laura. *The FBI's Most Wanted.* Broomall, PA: Chelsea House, 1997.

Kronenwetter, Michael. *The FBI and Law Enforcement Agencies of the United States.* Berkeley Heights, NJ: Enslow, 1997.

Streissguth, Thomas. *J. Edgar Hoover: Powerful FBI Director.* Berkeley Heights, NJ: Enslow, 2002.

ORGANIZATIONS AND ONLINE SITES

FBI Field Offices
http://www.fbi.gov/contact/fo.fo.htm

FBI for Kids
http://www.fbi.gov/kids/kids.htm

In the Line of Duty
http://www.lineofduty.com/dutywanted.htm

J. Edgar Hoover Law Enforcement Museum
1733 Sixteenth Street
Washington, D.C. 20009

Index

Bold numbers indicate illustrations.

Applicant, 27, 28, 41

attorney general, 6, 41

Bacteria, 34, 36, 41

blackmail, 15, 41

Civil rights, 17, 18, 19

communist, 10, **16**, 16–18, 41, 44

Community Outreach Program, 37, 38, 39

computer crime, 30, **30**, 31

counterintelligence, 5, 41

Debate, 18, 42

discrimination, 8, 42

domestic terrorism, 31–34, 45

dormitory, 23, 42

Espionage, 8, 16, 18, 42

FBI Laboratory, **14**, 15, 22

FBI National Academy, 15, **23**, 23–24, **24**, 25, 44, 45

federal, 4, 7, 9, 12, 42

felony, 8, 42

fingerprint, 13, **13**, **26**, 27–28

Gangster, 15, **15**, 44

Hacking, 31, 42

Hall of Honor, 24

Hoover, J. Edgar, 11, **12**, 13, 15–17, 19, **19**, 40, **40**, 44–45

Identification Division, 13, 44

intelligence, 5, 42

J. Edgar Hoover Building, 21, **21**, 22, **22**, 23, 45

Ku klux Klan, 10-11

Linguists, 37

Minorities, 18, 19, 20

NCIC 2000, 20, 45

Parole, 32, 33, 42

penitentiary, 13, 43

Pinkerton, Allan 5, **5**,

Pinkerton National Detective Agency, 5, 6, 44

profilers, 25, 26

prosecute, 9, 43

Recruit, 15, 43

Scandal, 11, 43

strike, 5, 43

suspect, 6, 9, 20, 26, 27, 32, 34, 43

Wiretap, 18, 43

women agents, 19, 20, **20**, 24

About the Author

In 1993 **Sarah De Capua** received her master of arts in teaching. Since then she has been educating children, first as a teacher and currently as an editor and author of children's books.

She has always been fascinated by the FBI and the detective work many of its agents perform to solve crimes.

Other books she has written for Children's Press include *Becoming a Citizen, Paying Taxes, Running for Public Office, Serving on a Jury,* and *Voting* (True Books); *J.C. Watts Jr.: Character Counts* (Community Builders); and several titles in the Rookie Read-About® Geography series.

Ms. De Capua lives in Colorado.